This is my...

Happy Birthday

...Perennial Cardbook

anthony j. gribin

© 2014

by Anthony J. Gribin

ISBN No. 97809827376-0-6
first edition

TTGpress

My name is:

My birth date is:

Introduction

Your birthday CardBook is an instant time capsule! The idea behind it is to gather well-wishes from people that care about you, over a long period of time. This card was given to you by someone important in your life; perhaps a spouse, partner, signifigant other, child, parent or close friend. It is similar to an autograph book at graduation; except the event of note is your birthday.

The more people that enter notes the better, and the more years the book is used, the better. Over time, you will be able to gauge how your children have matured as their entries change from bare legibility to adult sophistication; from stick figures to Rembrandt. Your CardBook should be left out at your birthday celebration, and all attending encouraged to sign.

The Cardbook will be "retired" after the celebration, put on a shelf, and "unretired" when the next birthday rolls around. If each member of your family has one, they can occupy a cozy spot together on a bookshelf and your family can "bond" even though no one is present.

There are 101 blank pages in each CardBook. 100 plus one for good luck. On the top of each page, you will see, "This is my____ Birthday, celebrated in ____." Enter the appropriate numbers, such as "45th" and "2014," to indicate that you celebrated your 45th birthday in 2014. It is unlikely that you will run out of room, yet it is possible if one or more celebrations are attended by, and the book is written in by, many people. Use as many pages as necessary for each birthday.

The CardBook can serve other purposes as well. Pictures can be pasted into the book as you wish. Annotations, either humorous or serious can be added. For example, "Uncle Joe was bombed when he wrote this," or "This was the last birthday that Mom was able to attend." You can make notes about who attended and where the celebration occurred. You can also mark down other happy occasions through the year, such as graduations, marriages or promotions.

The CardBook may replace individual yearly cards that, though they are nice to read in the moment, generally just collect dust afterwards until they are tossed to save space. Further, the often trite messages contained in store-bought cards cannot compare with a thoughtful and personal note written for you by a loved one. Reading "You mean more to me than ever..." written by a loved one is a lot more meaningful than reading it in a printed card. And by limiting the number of cards bought over the years, you will save money (on the cards themselves and the gas used to go to purchase them) and spare a few trees in the process.

After even one year of entries by multiple well-wishers, your CardBook will become an instant keepsake. It will aid remembrance of how you celebrated your birthday, who was there to share it with you and how the years have changed you. It is also a legacy for the next generation, to be put in the same category as old picture albums, videos and family trees.

And, by the way, HAPPY BIRTHDAY!

This is my ____ Birthday, in the year ____

This is my ____ Birthday, in the year ____

This is my ____ Birthday, in the year ____

This is my ____ Birthday, in the year ____

This is my ____ Birthday, in the year ____

This is my ____ Birthday, in the year ____

This is my ____ Birthday, in the year ____

This is my ____ Birthday, in the year ____

This is my ____ Birthday, in the year ____

This is my ____ Birthday, in the year ____

This is my ____ Birthday, in the year ____

This is my ____ Birthday, in the year ____

This is my ____ Birthday, in the year ____

This is my ____ Birthday, in the year ____

This is my ____ Birthday, in the year ____

This is my ____ Birthday, in the year ____

This is my ____ Birthday, in the year ____

This is my ____ Birthday, in the year ____

This is my ____ Birthday, in the year ____

This is my ____ Birthday, in the year ____

This is my ____ Birthday, in the year ____

This is my ____ Birthday, in the year ____

This is my ____ Birthday, in the year ____

This is my ____ Birthday, in the year ____

This is my ____ Birthday, in the year ____

This is my ____ Birthday, in the year ____

This is my ____ Birthday, in the year ____

This is my ____ Birthday, in the year ____

This is my ____ Birthday, in the year ____

This is my ____ Birthday, in the year ____

This is my ____ Birthday, in the year ____

This is my ____ Birthday, in the year ____

This is my ____ Birthday, in the year ____

This is my ____ Birthday, in the year ____

This is my ____ Birthday, in the year ____

This is my ____ Birthday, in the year ____

This is my ____ Birthday, in the year ____

This is my ____ Birthday, in the year ____

This is my ____ Birthday, in the year ____

This is my ____ Birthday, in the year ____

This is my ____ Birthday, in the year ____

This is my ____ Birthday, in the year ____

This is my ____ Birthday, in the year ____

This is my _____ Birthday, in the year _____

This is my ____ Birthday, in the year ____

This is my ____ Birthday, in the year ____

This is my ____ Birthday, in the year ____

This is my ____ Birthday, in the year ____

This is my ____ Birthday, in the year ____

This is my ____ Birthday, in the year ____

This is my ____ Birthday, in the year ____

This is my ____ Birthday, in the year ____

This is my ____ Birthday, in the year ____

This is my ____ Birthday, in the year ____

This is my ____ Birthday, in the year ____

This is my ____ Birthday, in the year ____

This is my ____ Birthday, in the year ____

This is my ____ Birthday, in the year ____

This is my ____ Birthday, in the year ____

This is my ____ Birthday, in the year ____

This is my ____ Birthday, in the year ____

This is my ____ Birthday, in the year ____

This is my ____ Birthday, in the year ____

This is my ____ Birthday, in the year ____

This is my ____ Birthday, in the year ____

This is my ____ Birthday, in the year ____

This is my ____ Birthday, in the year ____

This is my ____ Birthday, in the year ____

This is my ____ Birthday, in the year ____

This is my ____ Birthday, in the year ____

This is my ____ Birthday, in the year ____

This is my ____ Birthday, in the year ____

This is my ____ Birthday, in the year ____

This is my ____ Birthday, in the year ____

This is my ____ Birthday, in the year ____

This is my ____ Birthday, in the year ____

This is my ____ Birthday, in the year ____

This is my ____ Birthday, in the year ____

This is my ____ Birthday, in the year ____

This is my ____ Birthday, in the year ____

This is my ____ Birthday, in the year ____

This is my ____ Birthday, in the year ____

This is my ____ Birthday, in the year ____

This is my ____ Birthday, in the year ____

This is my ____ Birthday, in the year ____

This is my ____ Birthday, in the year ____

This is my ____ Birthday, in the year ____

This is my ____ Birthday, in the year ____

This is my ____ Birthday, in the year ____

This is my ____ Birthday, in the year ____

This is my ____ Birthday, in the year ____

This is my ____ Birthday, in the year ____

This is my ____ Birthday, in the year ____

This is my ____ Birthday, in the year ____

This is my ____ Birthday, in the year ____

This is my ____ Birthday, in the year ____

This is my ____ Birthday, in the year ____

This is my ____ Birthday, in the year ____

This is my ____ Birthday, in the year ____

This is my ____ Birthday, in the year ____

This is my ____ Birthday, in the year ____

www.ingramcontent.com/pod-product-compliance
Lightning Source LLC
Chambersburg PA
CBHW031325040426
42443CB00005B/214